HOCKEY TALK FOR BEGINNERS

HOCKEY

MESSNER BOOKS BY HOWARD LISS

HOCKEY TALK FOR BEGINNERS
BOWLING TALK FOR BEGINNERS
BASKETBALL TALK FOR BEGINNERS
FOOTBALL TALK FOR BEGINNERS
TRIPLE-CROWN WINNERS
ASGEIR OF ICELAND (with Ingeborg Lippmann)

TALK FOR BEGINNERS

by Howard Liss

Illustrated by Frank Robbins

JULIAN MESSNER
NEW YORK

Published by Julian Messner, a Division of Simon & Schuster Inc.
1 West 39 Street, New York, N.Y. 10018. All rights reserved.

Copyright © 1973 by Howard Liss

Printed in the United States of America

DESIGNED BY VIRGINIA M. SOULÉ

Second Printing, 1974

Library of Congress Cataloging in Publication Data

Liss, Howard.
    Hockey talk for beginners.

    SUMMARY: An alphabetical arrangement of hockey
terms with definitions, including "assist,"
"banana blade," and "zones."
    1. Hockey—Juvenile literature. [1. Hockey]
I. Robbins, Frank, 1917-   illus. II. Title.
GV847.25.L49 1973   796.9'62   73-7448
ISBN 0-671-32643-0
ISBN 0-671-32644-9 (lib. bdg.)

*For Pat and Jeff Shlan—who have taught me
what friendship really is*

HOCKEY TALK FOR BEGINNERS

ALL-STAR

A player selected to participate in the annual All-Star game.

ALL-STAR GAME

In January of every year, major-league hockey players compete in the All-Star game. The best players of the Eastern and Western Divisions are selected by members of the National Hockey League (NHL) Writers Association. The coaches of each team are permitted to choose additional players. The World Hockey Association (WHA) also has an All-Star game in midseason. (*See also* World Hockey Association.)

9

ART ROSS TROPHY

An annual award to the National Hockey League player who leads the league in scoring points at the end of the regular season. The trophy is given in honor of Arthur Howie Ross, one of hockey's early great players. He also was the manager-coach of the Boston Bruins. The trophy was first awarded in 1947.

ASSIST

A player is credited with an assist when he passes the puck to a teammate, and his teammate scores a goal. However, no more than two players can be credited with assists on any single goal. For example, if one player passes the puck to one of his teammates and the teammate passes to another teammate, who scores a goal, both players who passed will be credited with an assist.

ATTACK ZONE

The area between each team's blue line and the goal line. When the team in possession of the puck crosses the middle of the playing area and then moves across the defending team's blue line, the team with the puck is in the attack zone. (*See also* Blue Line.)

10

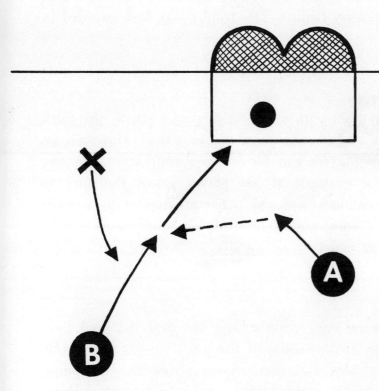

ASSIST

BACK CHECK

To skate back into your own defensive zone when your opponents have gained possession of the puck, and check an opponent as closely as possible.

BACKHAND SHOT

A shot or pass made with the back part of the stick's blade. It is something like "batting cross-handed" in baseball.

BACKHAND SHOT

BACK PASS

Passing the puck to a teammate who is coming up from be-hind the player in possession of the puck.

BAD MAN

Any hockey player who picks fights, checks much harder than necessary or joins a fight between two other players.

BANANA BLADE

A curved blade on a hockey stick. A few years ago, as Stan Mikita of the Chicago Black Hawks was practicing, he noticed that his shots were behaving strangely. The puck would dip down, sail up, or curve away. He saw that his stick's blade was cracked and bent. Later, other players tried bending their sticks by leaving them under a door overnight. But they were not always successful. Soon manufacturers began making sticks with curved blades, which the players called "banana blades." Hockey officials realized that this type of stick was giving offensive players too much of an advantage, so rules were made to reduce the curve in the blade. Today "banana blades" are not in use.

BENCH MINOR PENALTY

A player charged with a bench minor penalty must sit in the penalty box for two minutes. It differs from a minor penalty in that the person breaking the rules need not be the person who must sit in the penalty box. Rule 27 (b) states: "A Bench Minor penalty involves the removal from the ice of one player of the *team* against which the penalty is awarded, for a period of two minutes. *Any player* of the team may be named by the Manager or the Coach to serve that penalty."

For example, if a manager, trainer, team official, or executive uses profane language, or throws something on the ice, or tries to interfere with an official, the referee can impose a minor penalty. Since managers, trainers, and team executives are not players, they are not on the ice. Still, the team must be penalized. So a player is named to serve the penalty for two minutes. (*See also* Minor Penalty.)

BILL MASTERSON TROPHY

An annual award to "the National Hockey League player who best exemplifies the qualities of perseverance, sportsmanship, and dedication to hockey." A player must participate in at least fifty games to be eligible. The trophy is awarded in honor of Bill Masterson of the Minnesota North Stars.

BLUE LINE

The two lines dividing the attack zone from the neutral zone. Each line is one foot wide and 60 feet from each goal.

BOARDS

The wooden wall circling the rink. The boards can be between 40 and 48 inches high, but the ideal height is 42 inches. The smooth side of the wood must be facing the rink so that the players bumping into the boards will not pick up splinters or suffer other injury. The plastic or wire screens that protect the fans from flying pucks are mounted securely on the boards.

BOARD CHECK

To check an opposing player into the boards. Also called *boarding*.

OFFICIAL SIGNAL FOR BOARDING

BODY CHECK

BODY CHECK

When the player checks his opponent by using his hip or shoulder, or some other part of the body.

BREAK

The ability to start skating quickly, in any direction from a standing position.

BREAKAWAY

A swift rush by a player in possession of the puck. A breakaway enables a player to get away from his opponents, skate down the ice, and have a clear shot at the goal.

BUTT END

To jab an opponent with the top of the hockey stick. Very similar to *spearing*. It is illegal to jab an opponent in such a way. (*See* drawing on page 20.)

19

BUTT-END

CALDER TROPHY

An annual award to the player who is the most proficient in his first year of competition in the National Hockey League. The winner is selected by the NHL Hockey Writers Association. To be eligible, a player must not have played in more than twenty-five NHL games during the season. If the player tried to make the NHL team for two years before making the team, he must not have played in more than six games in each of those two years. From the 1936-37 hockey season until his death in 1943, Frank Calder, president of the NHL, donated the trophy. After he died, the league gave the trophy to the winning player. The first player to receive the Calder Trophy was Syl Apps of the Toronto Maple Leafs.

CARRY THE PUCK

To skate while in possession of the puck.

CENTER

One of the three regular offensive players. The center engages in the face-off at the start of each of the three playing periods and also after a goal has been scored. Such face-offs take place at center ice. (*See also* Face-off.)

CENTER ICE

The area of the playing rink between the two blue lines. Also called Neutral Zone. (*See also* Blue Line.)

CENTERING PASS

When a player in possession of the puck skating along one side of the rink passes the puck to a teammate who is closer to the center of the rink.

CHANGE ON THE FLY

To change the forward line while play is going on.

CHARGING

To charge across the ice in order to body-check an opponent.

It is illegal for the charging player to take more than two skating steps, and if he does, he will be penalized. It is also charging to making unnecessary contact with the opposing goalie.

CHECKING

There are three ways of checking—any kind of body contact, such as a body check or cross check; taking the puck away from an opponent; and guarding an opposing player.

CLARENCE CAMPBELL BOWL

This award is presented each year to the team finishing first in the Western Division of the NHL. It was first presented in 1968 in recognition of Clarence S. Campbell, who became President of the NHL in 1946.

CLEAR THE PUCK

To get the puck away from the area in front of the goal.

CRISSCROSS

An offensive play. The wingmen cross the ice and change sides. (*See also* Wingmen.)

CROSSBAR

The top section of the goal. It is a two-inch pipe, four feet off the ice, connected to the two side posts.

CROSS CHECK

CROSS CHECK

To check into an opponent with the stick while both hands are on the stick and no part of the stick is on the ice. A cross check is illegal.

CROSSOVER

A method of skating. The player skates over the ice alternately crossing one foot over the other.

OFFICIAL SIGNAL FOR CROSS CHECKING

DEFENSEMAN

One of two players on a hockey team who specialize in defensive play. They assist the goalkeeper in preventing opponents from scoring.

DEFENSIVE ZONE

The area between the blue line nearest to a team's own goal and their goal line.

DEKE

To feint or fake, trying to get an opponent out of position.

DELAYED PENALTIES

Although there are six men on each team, at least four must be on the ice at all times. But suppose two members of the team are already in the penalty box and a third player is charged with a penalty? In such a situation, the third player goes to the penalty box, and a substitute enters the game in his place. However, the penalty time that he must serve has really not yet started. As soon as one of the first two players in the penalty box is permitted to return to the ice, *then* the third player really begins to serve his penalty time. His substitute will leave the game so that, once more, the team has four players on the ice.

DRAG

Slowing down from a swift dash over the ice. To do so, one skate blade is "dragged" in a flat position.

DROP PASS

A form of backward pass. The player in possession of the puck skates forward, then suddenly leaves the puck for his teammate coming up behind him. Or he can nudge the puck gently back toward his trailing teammmate. (*See* drawing on page 28.)

DROP PASS

ELBOWING

Striking an opponent with the elbow. It is illegal. (*See* drawings on page 30.)

OFFICIAL SIGNAL FOR ELBOWING

ELBOWING

FACE-OFF

This is how play begins in hockey. Opposing players stand in one of the *face-off circles* (*see* Rink) with the blades of their sticks on the ice one foot apart. The referee drops the puck between the two stick blades, and the players try to gain possession themselves or pass to a teammate. (*See* drawing on page 32.)

FACE-OFF

FACE-OFF CIRCLE

One of five large circles on the ice where face-offs can occur. There is one circle at center ice and two circles in each of the attack zones.

FACE MASK

A protective mask worn by goalkeepers.

FLIP PASS

A type of pass that sends the puck a few inches above the ice so that the puck can "hop over" an opponent's stick. (*See* drawing on page 34.)

FOLLOW-IN

After a player takes a shot at the goal, it is good strategy for him to move quickly in toward the goal—to "follow in" his shot—so that he is in position to capture a rebound or a clearing pass.

FORECHECK

To check an opponent in his own defensive zone and prevent him from starting an offensive rush.

FOREHAND SHOT

The most natural kind of shot. A right-handed shooter has his left hand at the top of the stick, the right hand lower down on the shaft of the stick. This is reversed for left-handed players. (*See* drawing on page 35.)

FLIP PASS

FOREHAND SHOT

FORWARD

The forwards on a team are the left wing, the center, and the right wing. They are the players who generally lead the attack.

FORWARD LINE

Refers to the center and two forwards who form the attack

unit. Usually, a major-league hockey team has three forward lines, plus some spares who can fit into one of the forward lines. Often all three forwards will leave the game, to be replaced by a different forward line. That is because the members of each forward line usually practice as a unit, and each player is accustomed to the others' method of passing, feints, and skating habits. In the past, there have been many outstanding forward lines in hockey, such as the "Kid Line" of the Toronto Maple Leafs, featuring Charlie Conacher, Harvey "Busher" Jackson, and "Gentleman Joe" Primeau; the Canadiens' "Punch Line," consisting of Maurice "Rocket" Richard, Toe Blake, and Elmer Lach; Detroit's "Production Line" of Gordie Howe, Sid Abel, and Ted Lindsay; and Boston's "Kraut Line" of Milt Schmidt, "Porky" Dumart, and Bobby Bauer.

FREEZE THE PUCK

To maintain possession of the puck, passing it back and forth, but without attacking or trying for a goal. When a game is almost over and one team is holding a narrow lead, that team will try to hang onto, or freeze, the puck, keeping the other team from gaining possession, until the final buzzer sounds.

GOAL

There are two meanings for the term *goal*. Scoring a goal means passing the hockey puck into the "cage," which scores one point for the attacking team.

It also refers to the goal itself—the metal and nylon-net structure which is guarded by the goalkeeper.

The goals must be located ten feet from each end of the rink, in the center of a red line drawn across the width of the ice. The vertical goalposts are set into the ice. They are six feet apart and four feet high, and are joined by a crossbar. White nylon cord, usually referred to as the net, is attached to the frame. Automatic lights are wired to the goal, so that when a player scores, the light goes on.

GOAL

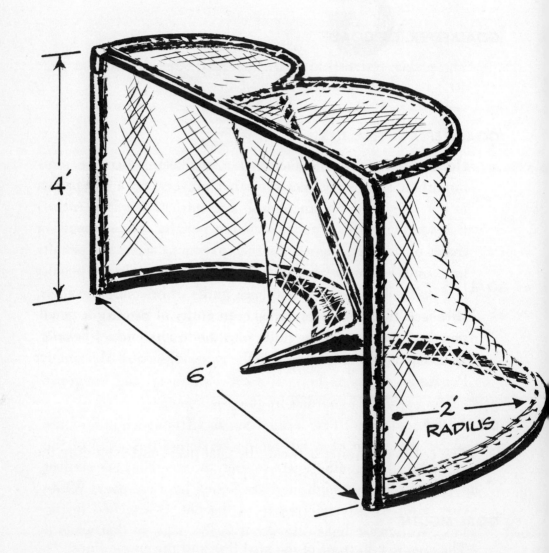

GOAL CREASE

An area in front of each goal, four feet by six feet, marked out with red lines. An offensive player who is not in possession of the puck cannot remain inside the goal crease. However, he is permitted to skate through the crease if he does have possession of the puck.

GOALKEEPER, OR GOALIE

The player assigned to guard the goal. (*See* drawing on page 40.)

GOALKEEPER'S PENALTIES

Hockey recognizes the fact that a goalkeeper may be more important to a team than the other players. So a goalkeeper is not penalized for an offense (or infraction of the rules) that would call for a major or minor penalty. The manager or coach of his team names another player to serve the penalty time, and the player who has been named must sit in the penalty box just as if he himself had been guilty of breaking the rules. However, if the goalkeeper has been guilty of two major penalties, he is automatically guilty of a *game misconduct penalty*. He is fined $50 and must leave the game. (*See also* Misconduct Penalty.)

GOAL LINE

The red line running between the goal posts and extending the width of the rink. (*See also* Goal.)

GOAL MOUTH

The area just in front of the goal line and the crease lines.

HARD STICK

When one player passes to another, the receiving player's stick should "give" somewhat, just the way a baseball player draws back his hand slightly when he makes a catch. "Hard stick" means that the player receiving the pass is holding his stick so tightly and rigidly that it does not move back at all. That makes control of the puck difficult, and sometimes it bounces off the receiver's stick blade.

41

HART MEMORIAL TROPHY

An annual award "to the player adjudged to be most valuable to his team." The winner, is selected in a poll by the National Hockey League Writers Association, receives $1,500. The player second in the poll receives $750. The Hart Trophy was first donated to the league in 1923 by Dr. David A. Hart, father of Cecil Hart, who was manager-coach of the Montreal Canadiens. It is now in the Hockey Hall of Fame at Toronto, Canada. The new Hart Memorial Trophy was presented to the NHL in 1960.

HAT TRICK

When a player scores three goals in a game, he has "turned the hat trick."

HELMET

Protective headgear. Few major league players wear them, but helmets are almost always worn by young players.

HIGH STICK

Carrying the hockey stick above shoulder level. (*See* drawings on pages 44 and 45.) High-sticking is illegal. If one player injures an opponent because of high-sticking, the referee *must* impose a major penalty on the offending player. The player is also automatically fined $25. (*See also* Major Penalty.)

HELMET

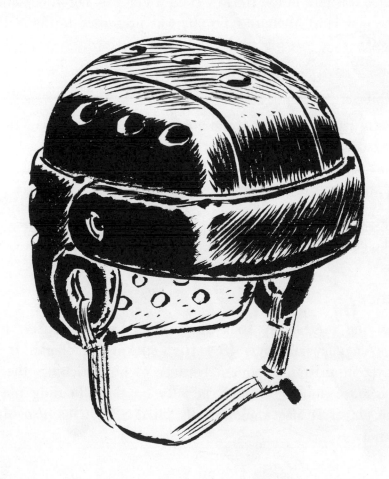

HIGH STICK

OFFICIAL SIGNAL FOR HIGH STICKING

HIP CHECK

HIP CHECK

To check an opponent with the hip.

HOCKEY HALL OF FAME

Most professional sports have a Hall of Fame building where fans can see pictures of all-time great players and the equipment they used and pore over statistics. Hockey's Hall of Fame was erected in 1961 and is located in Toronto, Canada.

HOCKEY TEAM

Consists of six positions: *goalie,* two *defensemen, center, left winger,* and *right winger.*

HOLDING

Using the hands illegally to hold or stop an opponent. (*See* drawings on pages 48 and 49.)

HOOK CHECK

A fast sweep of the stick close to the ice in an attempt to take the puck away from an opposing player. Also called *sweep check.*

HOOKING

Using the blade of the stick to hook or grip an opposing player from behind. Hooking is illegal, although a hook check is not. (*See* drawings on page 50.)

HOLDING

OFFICIAL SIGNAL FOR HOLDING

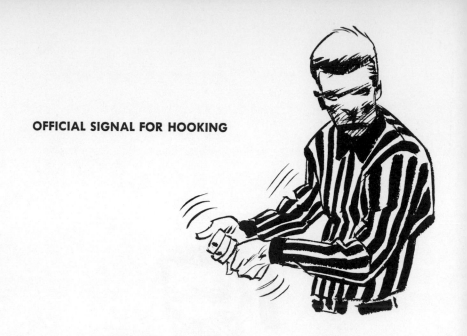

OFFICIAL SIGNAL FOR HOOKING

HOOKING

ICING (ICING THE PUCK)

Intentionally shooting the puck from behind the center red line, so that it passes through the other team's zone and over the goal line. The puck is brought back, and there is a face-off at one of the circles near the offending team's goal. (*See* drawings on pages 52 and 53.)

INTERFERENCE

To hinder a player moving down the ice if he does not have possession of the puck. This is called interference, and it is illegal. It is also considered interference if a player deliberately

ICING THE PUCK

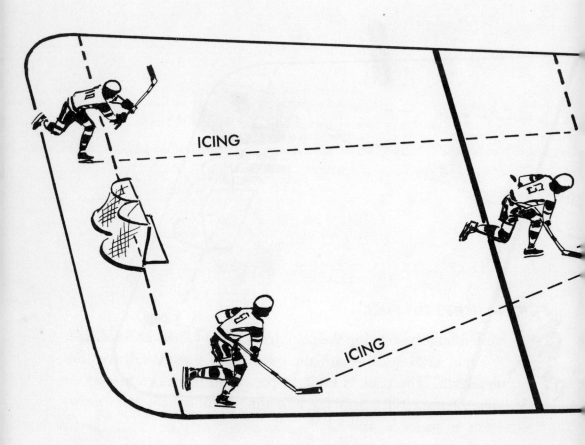

ICING

ICING

52

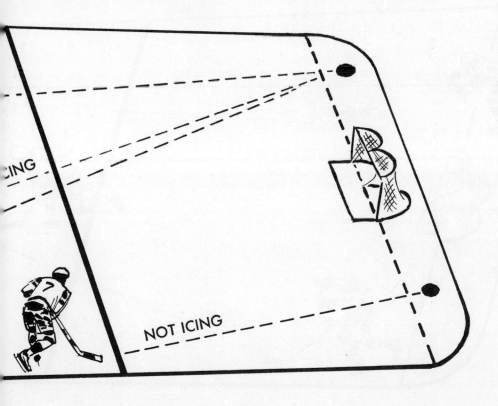

ICING

NOT ICING

knocks the stick from an opposing player's hands, or if he prevents a player who dropped his stick from picking it up. The referee will impose a minor penalty on the interfering player. (*See also* Minor Penalty.)

JAMES NORRIS TROPHY

An annual award "to the defense player who demonstrates throughout the season the greatest all-around ability in that position." The winner is selected by the National Hockey League Writers Association at the end of the regular schedule. The winner receives $1,500 and the runner-up $750. The award was first presented in 1953 in memory of James Norris by his four children. James Norris was the owner-president of the Detroit Red Wings. The first winner of the trophy was Red Kelly, who at that time played for the Detroit Red Wings.

KICKING (AN OPPONENT)

Any player who kicks or tries to kick an opponent during play receives a match penalty. At the end of five minutes, a substitute can play in place of the banished player. (*See also* Match Penalty.)

KICKING THE PUCK

It is legal to kick the puck during a game, but a goal cannot be scored on a kicked puck. However, if a player kicks the puck and it deflects off an opponent (any opposing player except the goalkeeper) into the net, then a goal is scored.

LADY BYNG MEMORIAL TROPHY

An annual award "to the player adjudged to have exhibited the best type of sportsmanship and gentlemanly conduct combined with a high standard of playing ability." The winner is selected by the National Hockey League Writers Association. The winner receives $1,500, the runner-up $750. Lady Byng, the wife of Canada's Governor-General, presented the trophy in 1925. After Frank Boucher of the New York Rangers had won the award seven times in eight seasons, he was given the trophy to keep and Lady Byng donated another trophy in 1936. After Lady Byng's death in 1949, the National Hockey

League presented a new trophy and changed the name to Lady Byng Memorial Trophy.

LEAGUES

No other sport has as many different organized leagues as hockey. No other sport starts a youngster playing so early as hockey. For example, the Parry Sound Community Center at Parry Sound, Ontario, Canada, permits youngsters of the area to compete in a great variety of organized hockey leagues, which are set up according to age. The *Minor Squirt* division is for boys five and six years old. The *Squirt* division is somewhat older, and then there are leagues called *PeeWee, Bantam, Midget, Junior,* and *Intermediate.*

There are *Senior* leagues for older amateur players, but the age limits may vary from town to town.

Of course, there are numerous other professional and amateur leagues throughout Canada and the United States, such as National Hockey League, World Hockey Association, American Hockey League, International-American Hockey League, Pacific Coast Hockey League, Quebec Hockey League, Eastern Professional Hockey League, Central Professional Hockey League.

LESTER PATRICK TROPHY

An annual award "for outstanding service to hockey in the United States." The winner can be an official, a coach, an executive, a referee, or a player. The winner is selected by a committee consisting of the President of the National Hockey League, a NHL Governor, a hockey writer for a U.S. national news service, a nationally syndicated sports columnist, a former player who has been elected to hockey's Hall of Fame, and a sports director for a U.S. national radio-television network. Except for the league president, the judges are changed yearly. More than one person can win the trophy in a year, but at least one of them must be living, while the other can receive it posthumously.

The trophy was first presented by the New York Rangers in 1966 to honor Lester Patrick, long-time general manager and coach of the Rangers. Lester Patrick and his brother, Frank, were great hockey players in the early 1900s, and they helped to organize the Pacific Coast League. The first winner of the Lester Patrick Trophy was J. J. "Jack" Adams.

LIE

The angle made by the shaft of the stick and the blade.

MAJOR PENALTY

A serious infraction of the rules, such as deliberately *spearing* or slashing an opponent. A major penalty calls for five minutes in the penalty box for the offending player. But it can be much more serious if the offending player hits an opponent on the face or head with his stick or continues to repeat the same kind of fouls. For example, the first time any player (except the goalkeeper) is charged with a major penalty, he is ruled off the ice for five minutes. No substitution is permitted for him during that time. Furthermore, if the offending player drew the penalty because he injured an opponent's face or head with his stick, he is automatically fined $25.

60

If the same player is charged with a second major penalty during the same game, he is ruled off the ice for fifteen minutes (five minutes for the major penalty plus ten minutes more for a misconduct penalty). A substitute can enter the game in his place after the first five minutes has passed. Any player charged with a second major penalty is automatically fined $25.

If the same player is charged with a third major penalty in the same game, he is ruled off the ice for the remainder of the game. A substitute can enter in his place after five minutes has passed. Any player charged with three major penalties in the same game is automatically fined $50. (*See also* Misconduct Penalty.)

MATCH PENALTY

Any penalty, or series of penalties, that will cause a player to be barred from the ice for the rest of the game.

MATCH MISCONDUCT PENALTY

When a player has been guilty of misconduct and is ordered off the ice for the rest of the game. (*See also* Misconduct Penalty.)

MINOR PENALTY

A two-minute penalty during which a player must sit in the penalty box. A minor penalty can be imposed by the referee for two reasons: either a player has broken one of hockey's rules or he has fouled an opponent.

For example, according to Rule 57 (a) of the Official Rule Book, if a player catches the puck in his hands and holds it, he has broken a rule and can be charged with a minor penalty.

If a player fouls, the referee must decide whether to impose a major penalty or a minor penalty on the player. Rule 47 (a) states: "A minor or major penalty shall be imposed on a player who runs or jumps into or charges an opponent." It all depends on how violently the player charged into his opponent. The same holds true for elbowing, butt-ending, cross-checking, etc.

MISCONDUCT PENALTY

A ten-minute penalty. There are many reasons for a referee to impose a misconduct penalty on a player. Among them are using bad or abusive language or showing lack of respect for the decisions of an official; banging on the boards with a hockey stick; refusing to go directly to the penalty box when ordered to do so by the referee; threatening to strike one of the officials; or if a player has been in a fight which has been broken up and tries to start the fight again.

NET

The nylon cord at the rear of the goal cage.

NETMINDER

Another name for goalkeeper.

NEUTRAL ZONE

The area of the hockey rink between the two blue lines.

OFFICIALS

In a National Hockey League game, eight officials are in charge of play: a *referee*, two *linesmen*, a *game timekeeper*, a *penalty timekeeper*, an *official scorer*, and two *goal judges*.

OFFICIAL SIGNALS

In hockey, officials use a set of hand and arm signals to inform players, coaches, and spectators of the progress of the game. Each signal has a special meaning. These illustrations show some of them. Others can be found on pages 17, 25, 30, 45, 49, 50, and 89.

CHARGING

CHARGING

DELAYED CALLING OF PENALTY

ICING

INTERFERENCE

MISCONDUCT

SLASHING

SLOW WHISTLE

WASHOUT

68

OFFSIDE

When an attacking player moves over the blue line into the attack zone without being in possession of the puck. Play is stopped and started again with a face-off. An offside is also called when a puck is passed over more than one line and becomes a two-line pass. (*See* drawing on page 70.)

OVERTIME

During the course of regular season play, a hockey game can end in a tie, and there is no overtime. But in the Stanley Cup play-offs, there must be a winner. If the teams are tied at the end of the game, play is continued after a face-off. The first team to score a goal wins. If 20 minutes elapses without a goal, an intermission is called. There is a short rest period; then another face-off takes place at center ice.

OFFSIDE AND OFFSIDE PASS

OFFSIDE

OFFSIDE

OFFSIDE PASS

ONSIDE PASS

PASS

When a player in possession of the puck sends the puck along the ice to a teammate.

PASSOUT

A pass by an attacking player from behind an opponent's goal to a teammate who is in front of the goal.

PENALTY

When a player or another member of a team (coach, trainer,

etc.) breaks the rules, he or his team is subject to a penalty. (*See also* Bench Minor Penalty, Delayed Penalties, Goalkeeper's Penalties, Major Penalty, Match Penalty, Match Misconduct Penalty, Minor Penalty, Misconduct Penalty.)

PENALTY BOX

An enclosed area just outside the rink where penalized players go when they are ordered off the ice. Also sometimes called the *banished box* or *jail*.

PENALTY KILLER

When a player is sent to the penalty box, his team is at a disadvantage because it has fewer players than the other team. The short-handed team often tries to keep possession of the puck until it is at full strength again. That is a job for the *penalty killers*. These players are adept at passing the puck to each other, avoiding checks, and keeping possession for their team until the penalized player can return to the ice. They have "killed" the penalty time.

PENALTY SHOT

A free shot on the goal. The player taking the shot picks up the puck at center ice, skates in on the goalie, and tries to fire the puck into the net. Only the goalkeeper is permitted to stop the shot. The penalty shooter gets only one shot. He is not permitted to take another shot if his first one misses and he gets the rebound.

Generally, a penalty shot is awarded to a player in possession of the puck, who moves into the attack zone and is then tripped or fouled from behind, or when some object, such as a stick, is thrown at the puck. If, because of such unfair actions, the attacking player does not score a goal, the referee can award him a penalty shot.

PERIOD

A hockey play period is 20 minutes. Three 20-minute periods make a hockey game.

POINT

The term *point* has two meanings in hockey. A team scores one point when a goal is made, or a player scores a point for his personal total when he makes a goal or an assist.

Point can also refer to the positions taken by players just inside their attack zone.

POKE CHECK

A quick thrust, or "poke," with the stick in order to knock the puck away from an opponent's stick. (*See* drawing on page 74.)

POLICEMAN

A player who deliberately roughs up an opponent, persists in being unnecessarily rough, or uses unfair tactics. In hockey, the *policeman* will check hard into the unfair player and sometimes even deliberately pick a fight.

POWER PLAY

When one team is short-handed because a player is in the penalty box, the opposing team will do its best to score a goal

by rushing as many players as possible against their outnumbered opponents. In this way, the attacking team will try to overpower its opponent.

PRINCE OF WALES TROPHY

This trophy is presented each year to the team finishing in first place in the Eastern Division of the National Hockey League at the end of the regular schedule. His Royal Highness the Prince of Wales donated the trophy to the National Hockey League in 1924. From 1928 to 1938 the award was presented to the team finishing first in what was then called the American Division. In 1939, when the National Hockey League had only one division, this trophy was presented to the team finishing in first place. When the NHL expanded in 1967, the trophy became a divisional award again, as it is today. The first team to win the Prince of Wales trophy was the Montreal Canadiens.

PUCK

An official hockey puck is made of vulcanized rubber. It is one inch thick and three inches in diameter, and weighs between five and one half and six ounces.

REBOUND

When the puck is passed or shot at the goal, it may strike the rink boards, an upright of the goal, or even another player. It will rebound off the object it strikes.

RED LINE

The line across the width of the rink which divides the playing area in half.

REFEREE

The official who controls the play.

REVERSING

To swing around while skating forward so that the skater is still going in the same direction but is now skating backwards.

RINK

A regulation hockey rink—the playing area for the game—is 200 feet long and 85 feet wide, with a red line dividing the playing area in half. The corners of the rink are rounded off. The rink is surrounded by a wooden wall or fence, known as the "boards," which, ideally, is 42 inches high (but not less than 40 inches high).

Ten feet from each end of the rink is a red *goal line* two inches wide. The goalposts are set into the ice on these lines. In front of each goal is a *goal crease,* marked out by 12-inch lines; the goal crease measures 4 feet by 6 feet. 60 feet from each goal line are the *blue lines,* which divide the rink into attack zones (and, of course, defensive zones) for each team. The area between the blue lines, also 60 feet long, is the *neutral zone.*

There are five face-off circles on a rink, two in each attack zone and one at center ice. In the center of each face-off circle are face-off spots. Four additional face-off spots, without any face-off circles, are in the neutral zone. Two are situated 5 feet away from each blue line.

RINK

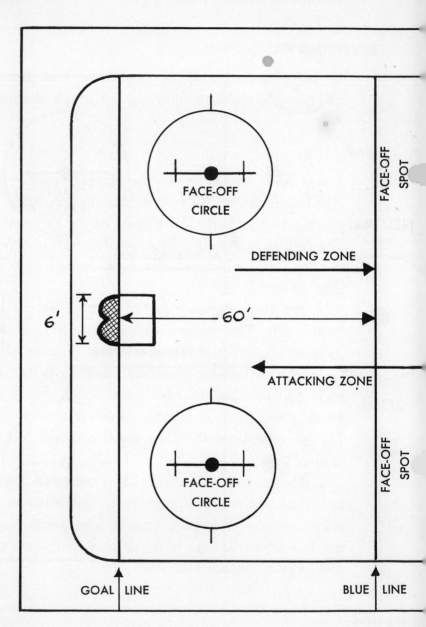

FACE-OFF SPOT

FACE-OFF CIRCLE

DEFENDING ZONE

6'   60'

ATTACKING ZONE

FACE-OFF SPOT

FACE-OFF CIRCLE

GOAL LINE   BLUE LINE

78

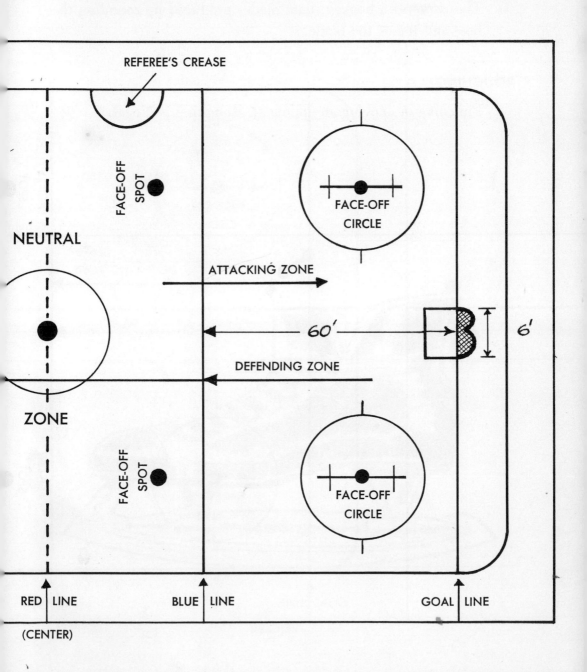

REFEREE'S CREASE

FACE-OFF SPOT

FACE-OFF CIRCLE

NEUTRAL

ATTACKING ZONE

60'

6'

DEFENDING ZONE

ZONE

FACE-OFF SPOT

FACE-OFF CIRCLE

RED LINE   BLUE LINE   GOAL LINE

(CENTER)

79

ROCKER

The curve of a hockey skate blade, produced by rounding the heel and toe of the blade.

ROUGHING

Punching or shoving an opponent. Roughing is illegal.

ROCKER

80

SAVE

Blocking of a shot by the goalkeeper. (*See* drawing on page 82.)

SCRAMBLE

Fast action when players bang into each other trying to gain possession of the puck.

SCORING CHAMPIONSHIP

The player who amasses the most points during a regular

SAVE

season wins the scoring championship. Points are awarded to a player (*not* to a team's total score in a game) if he is credited with an assist and, of course, if he scores a goal. (*See also* Assist.)

SCREEN

Any kind of action in which players are in front of the goal when an attacking player is trying to take a shot at the goal. Sometimes a goalkeeper's own teammates "screen out" his sight of the puck, so he cannot see when an opponent is shooting it. Or the shooter's teammates can screen out the goalkeeper's sight of the puck.

SHORTHANDED

When a team has fewer than six players on the ice because of penalties.

SHOT ON GOAL

When a player shoots the puck toward the goal cage.

SHOULDER CHECK

To check an opponent by using a shoulder.

SLAP SHOT

The slap shot is probably the fastest shot in hockey, sending the puck to speeds up to 110 miles an hour. It is executed by drawing back the stick with the bottom hand far down the stick. Then the stick swishes down and bangs the puck. (*See* drawing on page 84.)

SLASHING

Swinging the stick viciously at an opponent. Slashing is illegal.

SLOT

The area from about 12 to 18 feet in front of the net, between the two face-off circles.

SLOW ICE

Hard ice is best for hockey games. If the ice becomes watery or mushy, it slows the skaters and is called *slow ice*.

SLAP SHOT

SLOW WHISTLE

A decison that an official does *not* make, in order to keep the action going. If a player is offside as he goes across a blue line into his attack zone, the referee usually stops the game for a face-off in the offending team's defensive zone. But suppose, at that instant, the offside player's pass is intercepted, almost immediately after the offside has occurred.

To stop the action would be penalizing the team that regained possession of the puck. Therefore, the official gives the *slow whistle* signal—right arm, raised, other hand holding the whistle pointed downward. If the play returns to the neutral zone, the official drops his arm and the action continues.

SMOTHERING THE PUCK

When a player falls on the puck, he is said to be smothering the puck.

SNAKE

To whip or lash out at the puck with the stick.

SOLO DASH

A one-man rush toward the goal while in possession of the puck.

SPEARING

Jabbing an opponent with the stick. About the same as butt-ending. Spearing is illegal.

STANLEY CUP

A trophy awarded annually to the team winning the National Hockey League's final play-offs. In the quarterfinals of the play-offs, the team finishing the season in first place in each division plays a best-four-out-of-seven series against the fourth-place team, while the second- and third-place teams do the same. The winners of each division play a best-four-out-of-seven series against each other. Finally, the winner in the Eastern Division plays the winner of the Western Division in a best-four-out-of-seven series. The winner of that series takes possession of the Stanley Cup for the year.

STICK-HANDLE

Moving the puck along the ice with the blade of the hockey stick.

STICK LIFT

A defensive maneuver designed to prevent a shot at the goal. It can be particularly effective in front of the nets. A defensive player is beside the opponent who has the puck. Just before the attacker begins to shoot, the defensive player places his stick under the shooter's stick and lifts it.

SWEEP CHECK

Attempting to gain possession of the puck from an opponent by sweeping the stick in a half circle toward the puck.

SWEEP SHOT

To shoot the puck with a sweeping motion of the stick.

THREE ON TWO

When three attack players—usually the forwards—converge on the goal and only two defensive players are in position to stop them.

TIGHT TURN

To turn in a very short arc while skating.

TRIPPING

TRAILER

A player who follows his teammates on the attack, in position to take a drop pass. (*See also* Drop Pass.)

TRIPPING

To deliberately trip an opponent.

OFFICIAL SIGNAL FOR TRIPPING

TWO ON ONE

When two attack players converge on the goal and only one defensive player—the goalkeeper—is in position to stop them.

TWO-ON-ONE

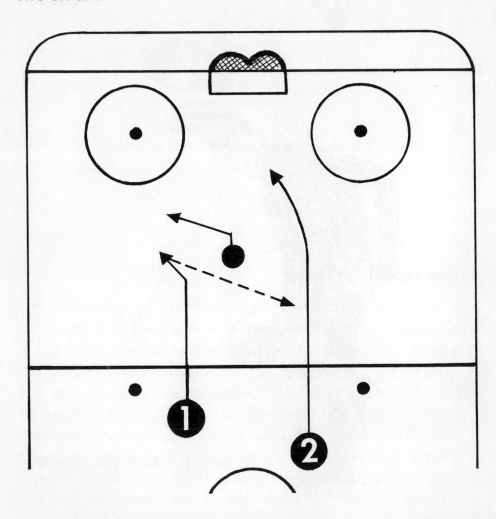

VEZINA TROPHY

An annual award "to the goalkeeper(s) having played in a minimum of twenty-five games for the team with the fewest goals scored against it." The winner is selected at the end of the regular season. The over-all winner receives $1,500 and the runner-up $750. The leader at the end of the first half of the season and the leader in the second half each receive $250. Leo Dandurand, Louis Letourneau, and Joe Cattarinich, former owners of the Montreal Canadiens, presented the trophy to the National Hockey League in 1927 in memory of Georges Vezina, outstanding goalkeeper of the Canadiens. The first winner of the award was George Hainsworth of the Montreal Canadiens.

WASHOUT

When the washout signal is given by the referee, it means that the goal scored has been disallowed, because of a penalty or some other infraction of the rules. When the washout signal is given by the linesman, it means that there is no icing of the puck or no offside. (*See also* Icing and Offside.)

WINGMEN

The two offensive forwards—right wing and left wing—who flank the center. Together they make up the complete attack unit. (*See also* Forward Line.)

WORLD HOCKEY ASSOCIATION

The World Hockey Association (WHA), which is now considered hockey's second major league, began operation in the 1972-73 season. Some of the new league's players quit their teams in the National Hockey League because they were offered a great deal of money to play for the WHA.

The WHA also has play-offs similar to those of the NHL, and an all-star game. It also started with two divisions. The East consists of Cleveland, New England, Philadelphia, New York, Ottawa, and Quebec. The West includes Winnipeg, Houston, Minnesota, Los Angeles, Alberta, and Chicago.

The New England Whalers defeated the Winnipeg Jets for the first WHA championship in 1973.

WRIST PASS

A pass executed by a quick flick of the wrist.

WRIST SHOT

Same as a wrist pass, except that much more force is used. A wrist shot can skim over the ice with great speed, although it is not usually as fast as a slap shot.

ZIGZAG

A series of crossover skating moves taken by the puck carrier so that he can avoid an opponent. (*See also* Crossover.)

ZONES

The three areas of a rink created by the blue lines. The attacking zone is that area farthest away from the goal a team is defending. Next comes the neutral zone, which is the area between the two blues lines, around center ice. Finally, there is the defending zone where the team's goal is located.

About the Author

HOWARD LISS was born in Brooklyn, New York, in 1922. He has written over thirty books, most of them in the area of sports. A few on baseball and football have been written in collaboration with such greats as Y. A. Tittle, Yogi Berra, and Willie Mays.

Mr. Liss considers it a "real labor of love to write sports books for young people."

About the Artist

FRANK ROBBINS was born in Boston, Massachusetts, on September 9, 1917. By the time he was fourteen, he had received two art scholarships.

Since then he has become a versatile and talented artist. He has exhibited in art shows, created comic strips and illustrated for advertising, magazines and books.